CHAIN

From Laughing Gas to Face Transplants

Discovering Transplant Surgery

John Farndon

Heinemann
LIBRARY

www.heinemann.co.uk/library

Visit our website to find out more information about Heinemann Library books.

To order:
 Phone 44 (0) 1865 888066
 Send a fax to 44 (0) 1865 314091

Visit the Heinemann Bookshop at www.heinemann.co.uk/library to browse our catalogue and order online.

Produced for Heinemann Library by
White-Thomson Publishing Ltd,
Bridgewater Business Centre,
210 High Street,
Lewes, East Sussex BN7 2NH

First published in Great Britain by Heinemann Library,
Jordan Hill, Oxford OX2 8EJ, part of Harcourt Education.
Heinemann Library is a registered trademark of Harcourt
Education Ltd.

Consultant: Professor Christopher Lawrence
Commissioning editor: Andrew Farrow
Editors: Richard Woodham and Kelly Davis
Proofreader: Catherine Clarke
Design: Tim Mayer
Picture research: Amy Sparks
Artwork: William Donohoe

Originated by RMW
Printed and bound in China by South China
Printing Company

ISBN 978 0 431 18597 2 (hardback)
10 09 08 07 06
10 9 8 7 6 5 4 3 2 1

ISBN 978 0 431 18604 7 (paperback)
11 10 09 08 07
10 9 8 7 6 5 4 3 2 1

British Library Cataloguing in Publication Data
Farndon, John
From laughing gas to face transplants : discovering
transplant surgery. - (Chain reactions)
617.9'54
A full catalogue record for this book is available from the
British Library.

Acknowledgements.
The author and publisher would like to thank the
following for allowing their pictures to be reproduced in
this publication:

The Art Archive p. 5 (Museo del Prado Madrid/Dagli Orti);
Corbis pp. 14–15 (Alison Wright), 21 (Bettmann), 25
(Bettmann), 27 (Jose Luis Paelaez Inc.), 29 (Bettmann), 40
(Bettmann), 42 (Reuters/Robert Pratta), 43 (Ruet
Stephane/Corbis Sygma), 44 (Reuters/Roland Quadrini),
46 (Bettmann), 48–49 (Reuters/Mike Theiler);
Popperfoto.com p. 19; Science Photo Library pp. 4, 6, 13,
18, 33 (SPL), 34 and title page (J.L. Marta/Publiphoto
Diffusion), 7 (John Bavosi), 8 (Eye of Science), 9 (Tek
Image), 10 (Pascal Goetgheluck), 11 (NIH/Custom
Medical Stock Photo), 12 (AJ Photo), 22 (Steve
Gschmeissner), 23 (Alfred Pasieka), 24 (Hans-Ulrich
Osterwalder), 26 (Alfred Pasieka), 30 (CNRI), 32 (Coneyl
Jay), 35 (Russell Kightley), 36 (John Watney), 38 (Hank
Morgan), 50 (Peter Yates), 51 (James King-Holmes), 52
(Peter Yates), 53 (Klaus Guldbrandsen), 54 (Klaus
Guldbrandsen), cover (Victor Habbick Visions);
Topfoto.co.uk pp. 17 (Matthew Fearn), 31 (Fastfoto
Picture Library), 55 (Jeff Greenberg/The Image Works).

Cover design by Tim Mayer.

Every effort has been made to contact copyright holders
of any material reproduced in this book. Any omissions
will be rectified in subsequent printings if notice is given
to the publishers.

Contents

Any words appearing in the text in bold, **like this**, are explained in the Glossary.

Replacing body parts

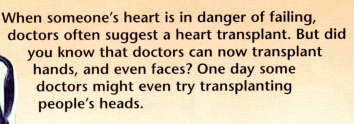

When someone's heart is in danger of failing, doctors often suggest a heart transplant. But did you know that doctors can now transplant hands, and even faces? One day some doctors might even try transplanting people's heads.

Just as a car often has faulty parts that need to be replaced, so do our bodies. Transplant surgery means replacing failing body parts with healthy ones. Sometimes it is only **tissues**, such as blood and skin, which are transplanted. Sometimes it is a whole **organ**, such as a liver, a kidney, or even a heart.

Organ transplantation is an old idea that dates back to the days of ancient Egypt. Yet it is only quite recently that these operations have become possible. Surgeons can now perform transplants to save the lives of many people who would otherwise die.

The story of transplants

The story of transplants is dramatic – full of spectacular triumphs and terrible tragedies. Not so long ago, nearly every patient receiving a transplant was almost certain to die.

This book tells how surgeons overcame all the obstacles to transplant surgery. It shows how they beat the body's tendency to damage the transplanted organ. It describes how they found ways to keep patients alive during the operation. It also explains how they learned to rejoin all the **veins** and **arteries** that had to be cut to perform the transplant. One great breakthrough led to another, until eventually surgeons could look transplant patients in the eye and promise them a good chance of a long and healthy life.

A scanner reveals some of the body's major organs, including the heart (pink) and the lungs (green). Both of these organs can now be transplanted.

Yet the story does not end there. Now surgeons are working towards transplanting entire limbs and even heads. In the future, it may be possible to replace any faulty body part with an entirely new part that has been made in a factory or grown in a laboratory.

This is how the painter Fra Angelico imagined Saint Cosmas and Saint Damian transplanting the Moor's leg. The picture was painted in Italy in the 15th century.

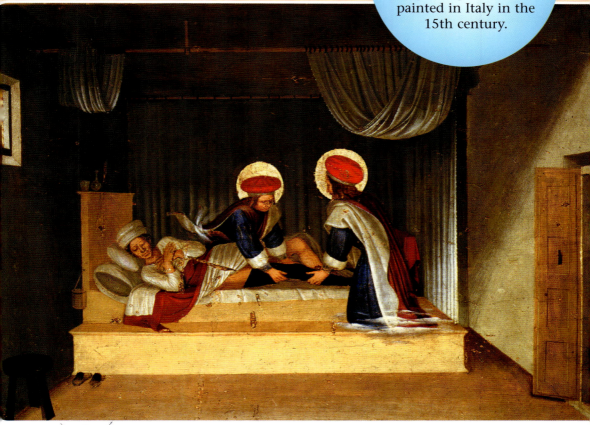

THAT'S AMAZING!

Limb transplants may not be as new as you think. According to a Roman legend, twin brothers Saint Cosmas and Saint Damian did a transplant operation way back in the 4th century in Asia Minor (now Turkey). Legend has it that Bishop Justinian was suffering blood poisoning in his leg and was likely to die. Miraculously, the saints replaced his poisoned leg with the leg of a dead Moor (a north-African). The bishop is said to have survived with one black leg and one white. The story was a popular subject for painters in the Middle Ages.

Early transplants

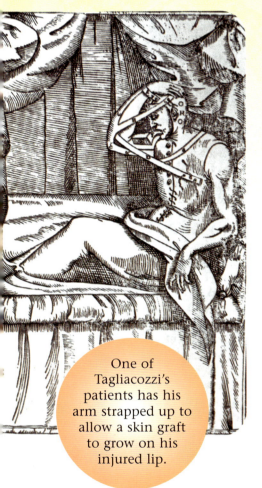

One of Tagliacozzi's patients has his arm strapped up to allow a skin graft to grow on his injured lip.

The first step in the chain of discoveries that led to transplant surgery was the skin **graft**. This is when skin from one part of the body is made to grow on another. Amazingly, surgeons in India learned how to do skin grafts thousands of years ago.

In ancient India, criminals were sometimes punished by having their noses sliced off. But a surgeon called Susruta found that he could rebuild a person's nose using a flap of skin taken from their forehead. The flap had to be kept attached to the forehead for a few days. This gave it time to "take", or grow its own blood supply.

In 16th-century Italy, Gasparo Tagliacozzi (1545–1599) used a similar technique to that invented by Susruta. However, Tagliacozzi took the skin from the person's arm rather than the forehead. The patient then had to spend a week with their arm strapped to their head while the skin graft took.

ETHEL SMITH'S STORY

In 1912, a young girl called Ethel Smith from Gary, Indiana, in the United States, was badly burned in a motorcycle crash. Local newsboy Willie Rugh generously offered the skin from his **polio**-damaged leg to cover her burns, even though taking the skin involved amputating his leg. Sadly, Willie died after the operation. Worse still, Ethel's body **rejected** his skin. Doctors did not know then that the transplant would only work if the **donor** and patient were related (members of the same family). In the end, Ethel was given several small grafts from her family.

Skin to skin

In 1804 another Italian, Giuseppi Baronio, made a further discovery. He found that if the graft was small, there was no need to keep both ends attached while it grew a blood supply. About 70 years later, Carl Thiersch (1822–1895) showed that if you cut skin thinly, to exactly the right depth, large areas could be cut off and grafted. For the first time, people with extensive burns could be helped with skin grafts. Thiersch's technique is still used today.

This diagram shows a cross section through human skin, greatly magnified.

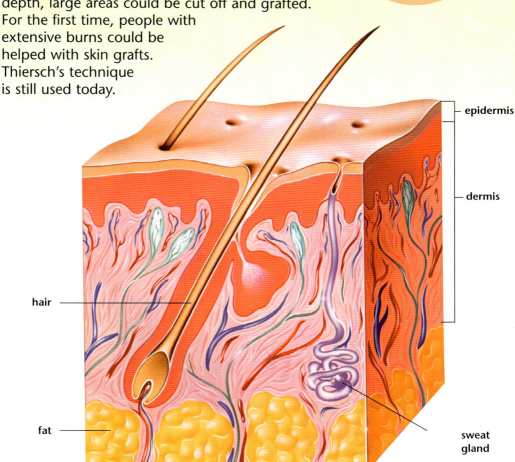

epidermis

dermis

hair

fat

sweat gland

![?] **HOW MANY LAYERS OF SKIN DO WE HAVE?**

Over most of our bodies, the skin is just 2 millimetres thick and can easily be cut with a sharp edge. Under a microscope, we can see that the skin has two main layers. On top there is a thin, outer layer called the epidermis. Below that, there is a thicker, lower layer called the dermis. The dermis contains glands such as sweat glands.

Blood transfusions

Another early form of transplant was a blood **transfusion**, when a patient is given someone else's blood. In the mid-17th century, French scientists were experimenting with blood transfusions between animals. Then, in 1667, a French doctor called Jean-Baptiste Denys gave a patient a transfusion of lamb's blood. The patient died and Dr. Denys was arrested for murder.

In 1819, there was an important breakthrough. London doctor James Blundell saved the life of a mother who was bleeding to death after giving birth. Blundell took some blood from his assistant's arm with a syringe, and injected it into the woman. This was the first successful human blood transfusion.

? WHAT ARE BLOOD GROUPS?

Your blood group is the type of blood you have. If you need a transfusion, it has to be the right group. It all depends on special chemicals in the blood: **antigens** on the red blood cells, and **antibodies** in the blood fluid or **plasma**. There are four main groups: A, B, AB, and O. Each group is divided into those that have a Rhesus antigen on their red blood cells (known as Rh positive) and those that do not have a Rhesus antigen (known as Rh negative).

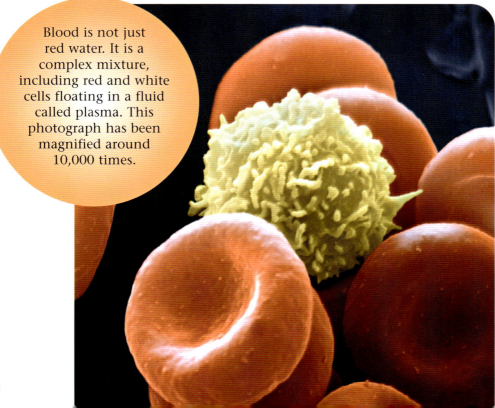

Blood is not just red water. It is a complex mixture, including red and white cells floating in a fluid called plasma. This photograph has been magnified around 10,000 times.

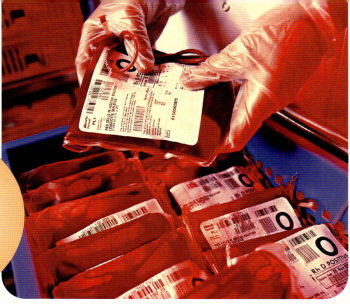

Blood is stored in cool conditions, in sealed plastic bags that are carefully labelled for type.

Matching blood

Blundell went on to give many more transfusions to patients who had lost a lot of blood. Yet the transfusions did not always work. Often the blood seemed to turn into a poison and kill the patient. Then it became clear that those who died were being given the wrong type of blood. In 1901, Austrian doctor Karl Landsteiner (1868–1943) showed that blood is not all the same. Instead, each person's blood is a particular type or **blood group**. A transfusion only works if the patient is given blood from the right group. This is why today, before a transfusion, the patient's blood is tested to ensure that the new blood matches.

Major operations often involve huge blood loss. The ability to make up this loss with transfusions was a major step towards successful organ transplants.

WHAT ARE BLOOD BANKS?

Early blood transfusions involved the donor and patient lying side by side with their **veins** linked by tubes. Then, during the First World War (1914–1918), doctors discovered how to store blood in containers. In 1917, before the terrible battle of Cambrai, in France, the doctors set up stores of blood ready to give to wounded soldiers. Nearly all blood for transfusions now comes from blood banks.

Corneal transplants

Sometimes people go blind because there is something wrong with their **cornea**, the clear layer that covers the eye. This can be damaged in an accident, or clouded by disease. In the early 1800s, doctors began to wonder if they could restore sight with a transplant. What if they could simply slice the patient's cornea off and replace it with one taken from a donor?

In 1838, Richard Kissam transplanted a gazelle's cornea into another gazelle's eye. A year later, he tried transplanting a pig's cornea into a human patient's eye. In both cases, the transplanted cornea clouded over and began to dissolve in a few weeks. Again and again, over the next 66 years, doctors tried to put animal corneas in human eyes, without success.

THAT'S AMAZING!

The cornea is rather like the glass that covers a watch. Because it has no **blood vessels**, it is completely clear. It is also extremely sensitive. There are more **nerve** endings in your cornea than anywhere else in your body.

Cornea-harvesting robots may be used to cut the cornea perfectly and quickly for transplant from the donor.

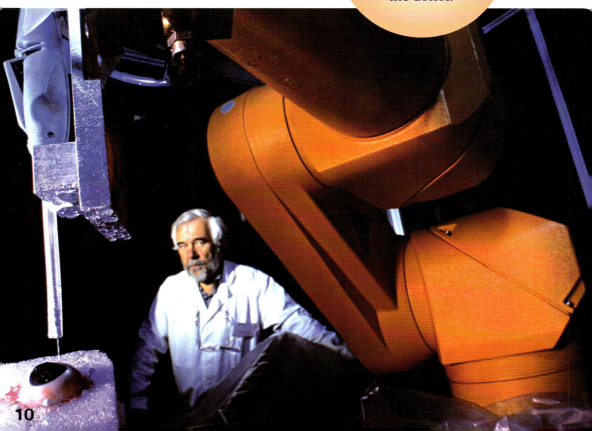

Eye to eye

In 1905, Austrian eye specialist Dr. Eduard Zirm was confronted with two patients. One was Czech farm worker Alois Glogar, who had been blinded in a fire. The other was Karl Brauer, a boy whose eyes had been damaged beyond repair in an accident. Dr. Zirm could not save Brauer's sight. So he cut away his undamaged corneas, and transplanted them into Glogar's eyes. Within a few hours, Glogar could see perfectly through one eye, and did so for the rest of his life.

Zirm's success led doctors to believe they could make transplants of other body parts from unrelated donors. The results were often fatal. What they did not know was that the cornea is a special case. The body's defences against foreign **tissue** are carried in the blood. Since the cornea has no blood supply, these defences have no effect here.

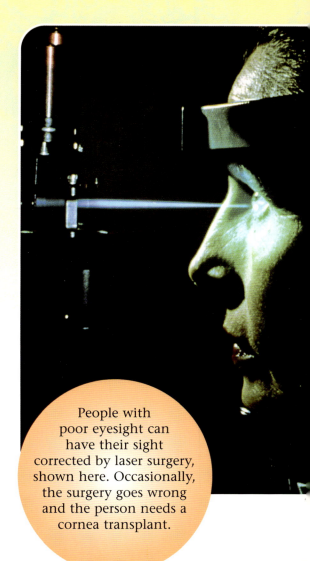

People with poor eyesight can have their sight corrected by laser surgery, shown here. Occasionally, the surgery goes wrong and the person needs a cornea transplant.

? HOW DOES AN ARTIFICIAL EYE WORK?

People sometimes go blind from damage to the **retina**. The retina is the light-sensitive area at the back of the eye. This is where the eye registers its picture of the world, then turns the picture into nerve signals to send to the brain. Doctors are now trying to implant completely artificial retinas. The patient has to wear special glasses with a tiny video camera fitted to them. The video camera feeds the picture (in the form of electric signals) to the implanted retina. The artificial retina then stimulates the nerves to send the picture (as nerve signals) to the brain. However, this technology is still at a very early stage.

Surgical skills

Before they could attempt **organ** transplants, surgeons needed to learn how to operate inside the body. The first vital step was the discovery of **anaesthetics**. General anaesthetics are chemicals that send a patient to sleep during an operation and stop them feeling pain. Local anaesthetics dull pain in one part of the body.

Before anaesthetics were discovered, the main operations surgeons did were **amputations**. These were horrible experiences for the patients. They were given alcoholic drinks and a gag was placed in their mouths, to stop them biting off their tongues in agony.

Operating on internal organs was out of the question. The pain of a long operation would be unbearable. Also, the muscles would stiffen in reaction to the surgeon's knife and make his task impossible. This meant that anaesthetics were needed, not only to stop the patient feeling pain, but also to relax the muscles.

Today, anaesthetists give patients an anaesthetic before an operation.

Sleeping through it

The first effective anaesthetic was the gas nitrous oxide, discovered by the English chemist Joseph Priestley in the 1770s. Another English scientist, Humphry Davy, called it "laughing gas" because breathing it in made people giggle. He suggested that it might relieve pain. In the 1840s, an American dentist, Horace Wells, used laughing gas to make taking teeth out less painful. He filled a pig's bladder with the gas and fed the gas to patients through a tube.

Wells' former partner William Morton (1819–1868) may have performed the first major operation under anaesthetic. Another American surgeon, Crawford Long, later claimed to have beaten him to it. But Morton's breakthrough became famous. Instead of laughing gas, Morton used a fluid called ether. The operation was carried out on 16 October 1846, at Massachusetts General Hospital in Boston, in the United States. The patient was Gilbert Abbot, a young man with a small **tumour** on his neck. Morton gave Gilbert fumes of ether from a bottle. Moments after breathing in the ether, Gilbert was asleep. The surgeon, John Collins Warren, quickly cut out the tumour. Half an hour later, Gilbert woke up, unaware that the operation had been done.

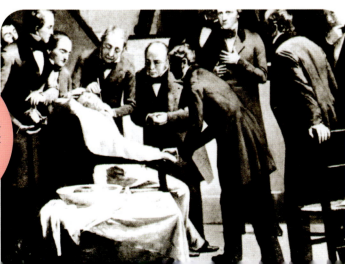

This illustration shows John Collins Warren operating on Gilbert Abbot, in front of an audience.

Powerful anaesthetics

Ether and laughing gas usually worked well for simple operations. But for major transplants, surgeons would need to find a way of keeping the patient asleep much longer. In 1847, Scottish professor James Simpson had the idea of using the vapour made by a liquid called chloroform. Sniffing a few drops of chloroform sprinkled on a cloth was usually enough to send the patient to sleep.

Laughing gas, ether, and chloroform soon became the main anaesthetics for surgery. Yet each had its own problems. Laughing gas kept the patient asleep only long enough for a quick dental operation. Ether took a long time to work, and made the patient throw up. It also tended to catch fire easily, which made it dangerous to handle and store. Chloroform often killed the patient with a heart attack. Worst of all, if patients were given a dose of ether or chloroform strong enough for transplant surgery, they would probably never wake up again!

HOW DID A BOMB LEAD TO A NEW ANAESTHETIC?

During the Second World War (1939–1945), some American scientists were trying to make the first atomic bomb. They needed to find special chemicals to keep the atomic reaction under control. While carrying out their research, they discovered a process called halogenation. This involves gases such as fluorine and xenon. A few years later, halogenation was used to produce a new anaesthetic called halothane. Halothane was much safer than ether and soon became very popular with anaesthetists. Anaesthetics developed from halothane are now widely used in transplant surgery.

In the 1940s, Canadian surgeon Harold Griffiths had a brainwave. Why not give his patients curare? Curare is a poison that some South American natives put on their arrows. The curare paralyses the animals the natives hunt so they can be caught. Griffiths knew curare worked by relaxing the muscles. If he could use curare to relax a patient's muscles, he could then use a much lighter dose of anaesthetic. He made a safe version of curare called intracostin. On 23 January 1942, he tried out his method on a patient who was having his appendix out. It worked. Now, similar muscle relaxants are routinely used in hospitals for all major transplant operations.

A Yagua Indian in the Amazon Basin, Peru, puts curare poison on darts used for hunting.

Learning from animals

With proper anaesthetics, doctors could at last try major operations. Yet before they could try human organ transplants, they had to be sure that they knew exactly how to carry out these operations. Gradually, they worked out, and improved, all their basic skills by operating on animals.

With anaesthetics, they could operate on unconscious animals. Around 1900, Hungarian surgeon Emerich Ullmann (1861–1937) did the world's first kidney transplant. The patient was a dog. Ullmann did not give the dog another dog's kidney. Instead, he simply moved the kidney from its body up to its neck. The repositioned kidney drained through metal tubes.

Further experiments repeatedly showed Ullman that transplanting a kidney from another animal never worked, even with an animal of the same kind. The transplanted organ was always **rejected**.

IS IT EVER RIGHT TO EXPERIMENT ON ANIMALS?

Over the centuries, scientists have conducted countless experiments on animals. The first transplants all involved animals. Many died or were cut up in gruesome ways, especially dogs, sheep, cats, rabbits, and monkeys. But, in the late 19th century, many people began to feel that experimenting on animals was cruel. They tried to get laws passed to prevent scientists carrying out some of these experiments. Today, many experiments are banned because they could cause animals to suffer. Animal experiments have provided a huge amount of knowledge that has saved many human lives through transplants. Yet the rights and wrongs of experimenting on animals continue to be fiercely debated.

LOLLIPOP'S STORY

A dog called Lollipop was one of the luckier animals in the early transplant experiments. Lollipop was the first animal patient ever to survive a kidney transplant from another unrelated animal. The **donor** was another dog and the operation was carried out in the early 1960s by Roy Calne, a British surgeon. Roy Calne successfully used drugs to prevent Lollipop's body rejecting the transplanted kidney. This was a breakthrough in transplant surgery (see page 29).

Heart moving

The remarkable French surgeon Alexis Carrel (1873–1944) was working on animal transplants at around the same time as Ullman. He also transplanted dogs' kidneys to their necks. Yet he could never transplant a kidney from another animal. He even transplanted a dog's heart to its neck. The dog died within a few hours, but Carrel was developing vital surgical techniques. Without these techniques, human transplants could never have been achieved.

People who are opposed to the use of animals for research sometimes hold protests like the one shown here.

LABORATORY ANIMALS NEED YOUR HELP

BORN TO DIE

Reconnecting blood vessels

The experiments on animals showed up a key problem. All the body's organs are supplied with blood through tubes called **blood vessels**. When an organ is cut out and replaced with a transplant, all the blood vessels must be carefully reattached.

If a plumber replaces a central heating boiler, he can easily reconnect the pipework with metal joints. But reconnecting the "pipework" for the heart or any other organ is much more difficult, because blood vessels are soft, living tissue.

Sewing blood vessels

The man who found the answer was Alexis Carrel, the doctor who had transplanted the heart of a dog in the 1890s. In 1894, the French president Sadi-Carnot was attacked and stabbed in Lyon, in France. One of the president's major **veins** was cut. His life could not be saved because doctors did not know how to repair the vein.

Alexis Carrel is seen here at work in his laboratory.

ELIZABETH MORROW'S STORY

Alexis Carrel also invented the world's first mechanical heart in 1935. He had a surprising helper, the famous American airman Charles Lindbergh. Carrel was treating Lindbergh's sister-in-law Elizabeth Morrow for a heart problem. To save her, Carrel would have to stop her heart for a short time while he operated. Yet stopping her heart would stop her blood circulating. Lindbergh asked if a mechanical pump might keep the circulation going. Carrel was already working on the idea, but was having problems. Then Lindbergh offered to help. His mechanical skills made all the difference. Soon the pair had built a heart pump that worked. Sadly, it was too late to save Elizabeth.

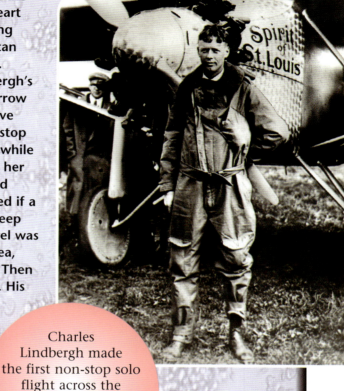

Charles Lindbergh made the first non-stop solo flight across the Atlantic, from New York to Paris, in 1927.

Carrel was determined to find a way to avoid such tragedies in future. He went to take lessons in sewing from Madame Leroidier, the finest embroiderer in Lyon. He practised for hours every day and became skilled at sewing with the tiniest needles.

Eventually, Carrel began experimenting on animals again. He worked out a way of reconnecting severed blood vessels. First he tied the ends loosely together in a triangle with three strands of silk thread. This held the blood vessels in place. Then he sewed the edges neatly together with tiny stitches. This technique, called "Carrel's **suture**", is used in organ transplants today.

Transplant rejection

By the 1940s, many surgeons had the skills to perform **organ** transplants. Yet these operations always ended with the patient dying. Then scientists discovered that this was because the body **rejected** the transplant.

Surgeons knew how to put new **tissues** or even new organs in place. But, again and again, the transplant failed. In particular, skin **grafts** rarely seemed to work if the skin came from anybody but the patient. In the Second World War, many pilots suffered horrific burns. They were left with very little undamaged skin to use for grafts. Yet skin from a **donor** was always rejected.

Rejecting transplants

British scientist Peter Medawar (1915–1987) was determined to find out why rejection happened. After experimenting on rabbits, he realized that bodies actively reject a foreign piece of skin.

The rejection process works like the body's defences against disease. When you catch measles, for instance, your body takes a few weeks to build up **antibodies** to the measles germs. Antibodies are proteins that attack particular germs. If you are exposed to measles germs again, though, your body remembers. It sends out armies of antibodies to start the fight against the germs straight away. This is why you never catch measles twice.

HOW DO CELLS RECOGNIZE EACH OTHER?

Every cell in your body has your own special identity marker. Only cells in the body of an identical twin, or occasionally a close relative, have the same marker. Australian scientist Sir Frank Macfarlane Burnet (1899–1985) realized that our bodies recognize these identity markers. In other words, your body knows which cells belong to you and so does not fight against them.

In the same way, the body accepts a skin graft from another body for a few weeks. Yet it knows the graft is foreign and begins to make antibodies. After a few weeks, it has made enough antibodies to fight against the intruder. This is why the graft is rejected.

WHAT'S IMMUNOLOGICAL TOLERANCE?

Peter Medawar found that grafts between identical twins are not rejected, because they are not recognized as foreign. This is called **immunological tolerance**. But if twins were the only people who could tolerate transplants from each other, how could doctors ever hope to perform transplants on anyone else? Then, in 1948, Medawar tried skin grafts on some cows. To his surprise, the grafts worked on a few unrelated cows. This made him realize that, because they are bred very closely together, unrelated cows could gain the same immunological tolerance as identical twins. The idea that the **immune system** could somehow be fooled proved vital to the future of transplant surgery.

Born in Brazil, Peter Medawar was the son of a Lebanese-British businessman and studied zoology at Oxford University. He was a joint Nobel Prize-winner in 1960 for his work on immunological tolerance.

The immune system

By the 1950s, scientists knew that the body rejected foreign tissue. What astonished them was just how intricate the body's defences were. On the surface, there are barriers to invaders. These barriers include the skin and the mucus lining the airways. Inside the body, there is also an amazing array of special cells whose only job is to target invaders. Together, they form the body's immune system.

White blood cells

The body's "big guns" are pale-coloured cells in the blood called **white blood cells**. Some white blood cells are much bigger than others. They are called **macrophages** and they simply swallow up invading germs. In the late 1950s, scientists discovered even more remarkable white blood cells. This type of cell can actually learn to recognize and target particular invaders. These targeting cells, called **lymphocytes**, are the cells that reject foreign transplants.

These white blood cells have been magnified around 4,750 times.

In the late 1950s, Frank Macfarlane Burnet showed how these targeting cells work. Whenever they meet an invader, such as a germ, they start to multiply rapidly. As they multiply, they send out floods of chemical markers called antibodies. These latch on to the invaders so that the body's defences (including macrophages and special killer lymphocytes) can recognize and attack them.

WHAT ARE B CELLS AND T CELLS?

There are two main types of lymphocyte: B cells and T cells. B cells are the ones that make antibodies. T cells are more actively aggressive. Some T cells are killer cells that dissolve invaders. Others latch on to cells marked by antibodies and encourage macrophages to swallow them up.

In this way, the body's immune system learns to target particular germs. The first time the antibodies meet a new invader, it takes a while for them to build up. However, the next time, and every time afterwards, they can multiply very quickly. This is why early transplants seemed to be accepted at first, but were then rejected, as antibodies built up and helped white blood cells attack the transplant.

Antibodies are like paint markers. They stick to an invading cell and destroy it, or signal that it needs to be destroyed by the body's defences.

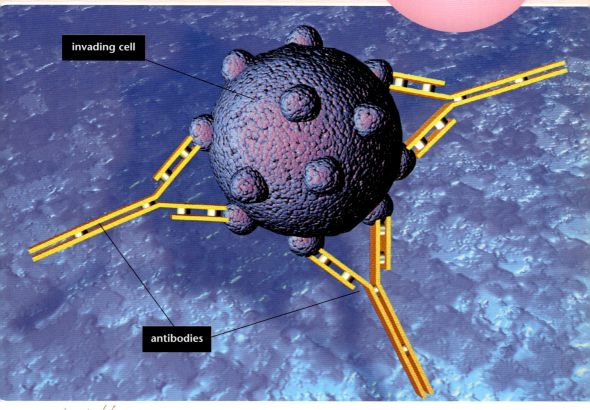

invading cell

antibodies

WHAT ARE ANTIBODIES AND ANTIGENS?

Every kind of germ or strange cell has chemical marks on its surface called **antigens.** Your body has antibodies for every antigen it has ever encountered. Antibodies are special Y-shaped proteins that stick their prongs into the invader. Some actively interfere with the invader's chemistry. Some simply identify it so that it can be targeted by macrophages and lymphocytes.

The first organ transplants

It took many years to find out why transplants were **rejected**. Nevertheless, desperate to save their patients' lives, doctors began to try **organ** transplants. The first organ they tried to transplant was the kidney.

To do a kidney transplant, doctors needed a machine that would take over the work of the patient's kidney for a short time. In 1938, a Dutch doctor called Willem Kolff saw a young patient die of kidney disease. Deeply upset by this, Kolff decided to find a way to beat kidney disease.

This diagram shows a slice through a kidney. Blood enters the kidney through the renal **artery** on the left. The nephrons filter out waste. The waste flows out with unwanted water as urine through the ureter.

Kidneys filter out waste from the blood. Kolff wanted to make a mechanical filter that took over from a damaged kidney. This machine would give the patient's kidney a chance to recover. This process is called **dialysis**.

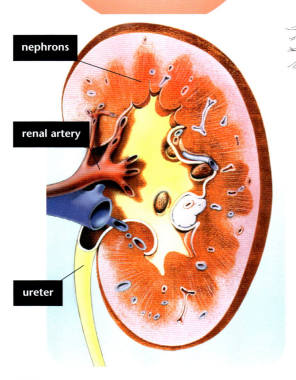

nephrons

renal artery

ureter

? WHAT DO THE KIDNEYS DO?

The kidneys clean the blood. They catch larger, unwanted materials, and let smaller, wanted, blood ingredients pass through. They also control the amount of water in the blood. They do this by soaking up all the wanted ingredients with just the right proportion of water. They then return the wanted ingredients and water to the bloodstream. All the waste material flows away with the unwanted water, as urine.

The first dialysis machine

Kolff was just starting his experiments when the Second World War broke out. The Nazis invaded the Netherlands and this made life dangerous for Kolff. He secretly built a dialysis machine, using any materials he could find. He pierced holes in sausage skin to make the filter. He collected orange juice cans to hold the blood. He used a washing-machine drum to whirl the blood round and fling it through the filter.

Kolff's machine was crude, but it worked. In 1945, he used it to treat an old woman who was dying of kidney disease. After 11 hours, the woman came round and said, "I'm going to divorce my husband." She did, and lived for many years after.

This 15-year-old patient is having dialysis in the mid-1960s, in the United States.

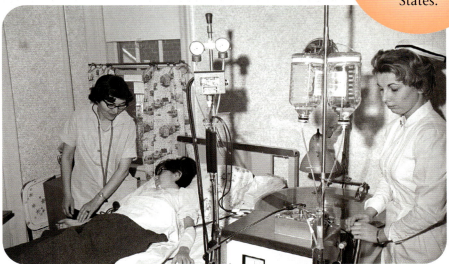

HOW DOES A DIALYSIS TAP WORK?

People with incurable kidney disease need frequent dialysis. A better version of Kolff's machine could provide this. But each time patients were connected to the machine, doctors had to put needles in their arms. Their blood vessels were soon damaged by all the needles. In the late 1950s, Dr. Belding Scribner found a solution. He put a tiny tap inside the patient's arm, made of a new material called Teflon (used to line non-stick saucepans). This tap, called a shunt, would never get rusty. It could also be connected to the dialysis machine easily via plastic pipes.

Kidneys for twins

Surgeons soon realized that Kolff's dialysis machine not only gave a damaged kidney time to recover, it also kept a patient alive during a transplant.

In 1952, a Parisian mother persuaded surgeon René Küss to transplant one of her two kidneys to her son. The son's own single kidney had been damaged in a fall. The patient was kept alive using the dialysis machine until the operation, and the surgery went well. Soon, the transplanted kidney began working. But less than two weeks later, the boy died.

medulla

ureter

medullary pyramids

This coloured scan shows a healthy human kidney. The urine drains through the medullary pyramids into the ureter, which leads to the bladder.

WHY DO LIVING PEOPLE DONATE KIDNEYS?

Most kidneys come from donors who have died. But a few come from living donors, who are generous enough to give up one of their two kidneys. People can manage with one kidney, and kidneys from living donors are in better condition. As they usually come from a relative, there is less chance of them being rejected. In the United Kingdom, 10 per cent of transplanted kidneys come from live donors. In the United States this figure is 25 per cent.

WHAT MAKES SOME TWINS IDENTICAL?

Some twins look exactly the same as each other. They are called identical twins. They are identical because they both come from a single egg, which split soon after it was fertilized. Non-identical (or fraternal) twins come from two separate eggs. Identical twins are always the same sex and have the same blood type.

Two of a kind

In 1954, at a hospital in Boston, in the United States, Joseph Murray performed the world's first successful organ transplant.

The patient was Richard Herrick and the **donor** was his twin brother Ronald. They were identical twins, so Murray felt there was a good chance that Richard's body would not reject Ronald's kidney. First, he tested the twins' **blood group** and found that it was identical. He also tried a small skin **graft** to see if that was rejected. That worked too, so on 23 December Murray decided to go ahead with the transplant.

The operation lasted three and a half hours. Murray took out Ronald's kidney in one operating room, and transplanted it into Richard in the room next door. To everyone's relief, the operation worked and the kidney went on working. Richard Herrick later married the nurse who looked after him in the recovery room. They had two children together, and Richard lived another eight years before dying of a heart attack.

Identical twins can donate organs to each other without fear of rejection.

Beating the body's defences

After Joseph Murray's success in Boston, other doctors also tried to transplant kidneys. Yet nearly every patient died, as the new kidney was **rejected**. Only transplants between identical twins ever worked. Doctors were desperate to find a solution.

At first, they tried to reduce the chances of rejection by weakening the body's **immune system**. They used lots of X-rays on the patient. But this weakened the immune system so much that even the mildest infection made the patient very ill.

Then American blood specialist William Dameshek thought of using an anti-cancer drug called 6-mp. Cancer cells do their damage by multiplying rapidly. This drug interfered with the cancer cells' chemistry to stop them multiplying. Scientists knew that transplant rejection begins when **white blood cells** multiply to fight the transplant. Dameshek thought 6-mp might prevent rejection by stopping white blood cells multiplying.

WHAT ARE STEROIDS?

Corticosteroids, or steroids, are one of the miracle drugs of the last century. When your body is injured or affected by an illness, your immune system often reacts by causing **inflammation**. Natural steroid chemicals in the body suppress this reaction. Steroid drugs are man-made versions of these chemicals. They are used to treat many illnesses, from asthma to rheumatism. Corticosteroids are not the same as anabolic steroids, which some athletes use illegally to make their muscles grow.

Double drugs

Experiments on rabbits showed that Dameshek was right. Then, in the early 1960s, British doctor Roy Calne tried out the idea with kidney transplants on dogs. After each transplant, he gave the dogs a similar drug to 6-mp, called **azathioprine**. It worked so well with a dog called Lollipop (see page 17) that Calne decided to try it with human transplants.

Calne's patients did better than earlier transplant patients. Yet still only a few survived. Then, in 1963, Thomas Starzl, in the United States, made a breakthrough. He gave all his transplant patients azathioprine. Whenever the transplant looked as if it was going to be rejected, he also gave them a huge dose of **steroid** drugs. The combination dramatically reduced the chances of a transplant being rejected. Because they suppress the body's immune system, these drugs are known as **immunosuppressants**.

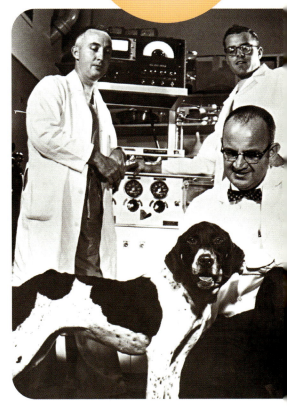

This dog, Sam, received a transplanted heart valve, in the 1960s at Stanford, in the United States.

THAT'S AMAZING!

Researchers at a Swiss drug company used to collect bags of soil to look for fungi. They were searching for fungi that might contain **antibiotic** substances. In the 1960s, they found a fungus called *Tolypocladium inflatum*. From it, they took a substance they called **cyclosporine**. This was tested and then finally approved for use in the early 1980s. Cyclosporine could suppress the immune system much more effectively than azathioprine. In fact, cyclosporine works so well that transplant patients given cyclosporine rarely need steroid treatment and recover much faster.

Tissue typing

Drugs that weakened the immune system made it much less likely that a transplant would be rejected. Yet the drugs did not always work, and they often made the patient quite ill. Scientists wanted to find ways to identify **donors** whose **organs** were less likely to be rejected.

Blood tests helped ensure that the donor and patient were the same **blood group**. But doctors needed to know more about how the body identifies foreign cells.

Chemical passports

In the 1960s, scientists found that there are special marker proteins in the coating of nearly every cell in the body. These proteins are called **human leukocyte antigens (HLAs)**. This is because they are especially common on white blood cells called leukocytes.

HLAs are the body's "chemical passports". From the pattern of HLAs on a cell, the body's immune system can instantly recognize which cells are its own and which are foreign. It is HLAs that mark out a transplanted organ as foreign and ensure that it is rejected.

This false-colour photograph of a human white blood cell (bottom) has been magnified around 26,400 times. The HLA antigen is shown as the uneven red areas on the outer surface of the cell.

Doctors began to realize that it was worth doing a blood test on donors to see how closely their HLAs matched those of the patient. This is called **tissue typing**. The closer the match, the less likely an organ is to be rejected.

ZAIN HASHMI'S STORY

Zain Hashmi is a young boy who suffers from a rare blood illness called thalassaemia. He is kept alive by blood **transfusions**, but to live long he needs a transplant of bone marrow from a perfect match. A baby brother or sister might be a perfect match, but there is only one way to be sure. The fertilized egg, from which the baby will grow, has to be tissue-typed first, to make sure it is a perfect match. Then the egg has to be artificially implanted into Mrs. Hashmi's womb. Before the baby is born, stem cells will be taken from the umbilical cord to help regenerate Zain's bone marrow. The Hashmis now have permission to do all this. But some people think it is wrong to create a new life with the aim of using cells from the baby's umbilical cord blood to cure its older brother – even though the new baby would not be harmed.

Zain Hashmi is shown here with his parents.

Pancreas and liver

Kidney damage is often linked to diabetes. This is a disease caused by a problem in an **organ** called the pancreas. Doctors doing the first kidney transplants wondered if it might be worth transplanting the pancreas at the same time.

WHERE DO DIABETICS GET INSULIN FROM?

For more than half a century, diabetics got their insulin from animals. Then, in 1980, scientists found a way of producing **genetically engineered** bacteria to make human insulin. They thought this would be much better than the animal insulin. However, many diabetics have found that natural animal insulin works better than genetically modified (GM) human insulin.

Diabetes is caused when the pancreas fails to make a **hormone** called **insulin**. Insulin circulates in the blood. It enables cells to take in the sugar they need from the blood, for energy. Without insulin, cells cannot take in sugar, and sugar levels in the blood can rise dangerously.

In the 1920s, doctors made a discovery. They could treat diabetics with regular injections of insulin, taken from animals. Injected insulin seemed to stop all the symptoms of the disease. But the slight excess of blood sugar eventually took its toll.

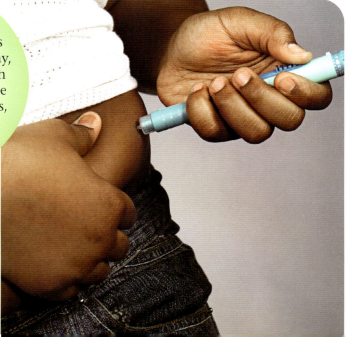

Diabetics need to inject themselves with insulin every day, often in the stomach but sometimes in the upper arms, buttocks, or thighs.

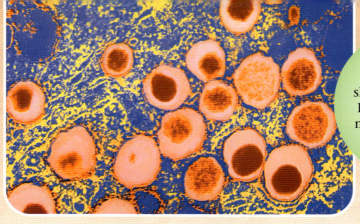

This photograph shows the islets of Langerhans cells, magnified around 19,200 times.

The patient's **blood vessels** became more and more damaged. Diabetics often went blind, or suffered kidney failure, or both. Indeed, diabetes became a very common reason for people needing to have a kidney transplant.

Pancreas transplants

It made no sense to give a diabetic person a kidney transplant if the new kidney was also going to be damaged by the disease. For this reason, doctors decided to try transplanting the pancreas at the same time as the kidney. A healthy pancreas might produce insulin properly. In 1967, Richard Lillehei carried out the world's first kidney and pancreas transplant at the University of Minnesota, in the United States.

At first, such double transplants were rarely successful because of problems with **rejection**. But the introduction of the drug **cyclosporine** (see page 29) made a huge difference. Now thousands of successful double transplant operations are performed each year.

? WHAT ARE ISLET TRANSPLANTS?

Insulin is made in the pancreas, in small clusters of cells called the islets of Langerhans. In the 1970s, doctors realized that they might be able to treat diabetes by transplanting just the islet cells and not the entire pancreas. Islet transplants are much easier to perform than a full pancreas transplant. These cell transplants are becoming more common and more successful. However, the patient has to stay on cyclosporine or **steroids** indefinitely.

Liver transplants

Once kidney transplants became more common, doctors began to wonder if they could also transplant livers. But livers proved much more difficult.

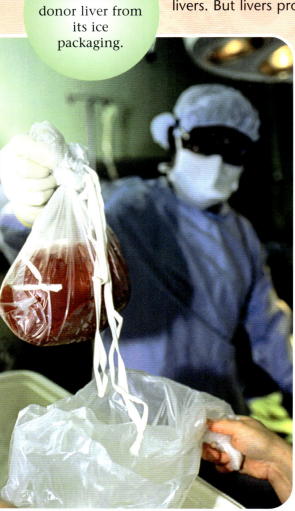

A surgeon removes a donor liver from its ice packaging.

Using a **dialysis** machine, patients could be kept alive long enough for a transplanted kidney to start working. But there was no such machine to replace the liver, which plays a vital role in the body by breaking down fats and removing toxins. The new liver had to start working at once, or the patient would die. The liver is also much bigger and harder to handle than a kidney. Worse still, the liver is very sensitive to a lack of blood supply. For this reason, the **donor** liver is ruined if it is not taken out and chilled within 15 minutes of the donor's death.

Despite all these problems, some doctors were willing to give liver transplants a try, because they had patients who would certainly die without them. In 1963, Thomas Starzl in the United States and Roy Calne in the United Kingdom both tried liver transplants.

? WHICH DISEASES DAMAGE THE LIVER?

There are a number of diseases that damage the liver. These diseases include cirrhosis and liver cancer. One of the major liver diseases is hepatitis. HCV is short for the hepatitis C virus. HCV is one of the most common blood infections in developed countries such as the United States. You catch it when your blood comes into contact with the blood of an infected person. If the damage to the patient's liver is severe, a liver transplant may be needed.

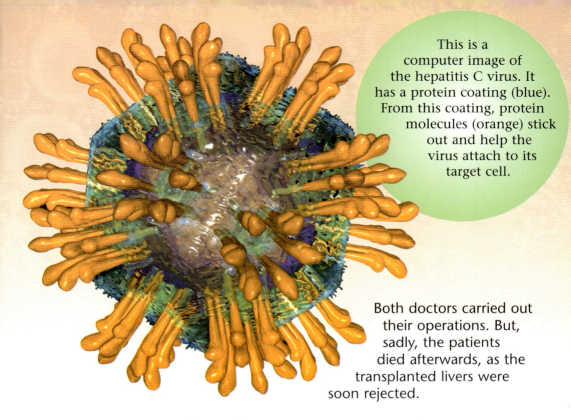

This is a computer image of the hepatitis C virus. It has a protein coating (blue). From this coating, protein molecules (orange) stick out and help the virus attach to its target cell.

Both doctors carried out their operations. But, sadly, the patients died afterwards, as the transplanted livers were soon rejected.

New livers

This remained the pattern for much of the next 20 years. Doctors got better at carrying out the transplant operations. But three out of every four patients still died within a year.

Then, in the early 1980s, Roy Calne began to use the drug cyclosporine to reduce the chances of the liver being rejected. The effects were dramatic. Soon, nine out of ten liver transplant patients survived at least a year after the operation. Many patients regained full health.

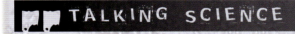

TALKING SCIENCE

"[Our] experiments gave us confidence in liver transplant operations in the pig, where the anatomy is similar to that of humans. All of this [animal] experimentation was, of course, the foothills; [human] liver transplant was our Everest, and Thomas Starzl was the first to scale it in 1963."

Sir Roy Calne, in his book *The Gift of Life*, on fellow liver transplant pioneer Thomas Starzl

New hearts for old

By the early 1960s, doctors had transplanted the kidney, pancreas, and liver. Now they started wondering if they could attempt the "Big One" – a heart transplant.

Without our hearts to pump blood and supply our bodies with oxygen, we quickly die. For this reason, heart transplants were going to be especially hard. Yet Norman Shumway and Richard Lower of Stanford University, in the United States, were determined to overcome the problems.

First, Shumway needed to find a way to stop the patient's old heart safely while it was taken out. He realized he could simply chill it with icy water to stop the blood flow. Next, he perfected an artificial heart machine to take over until the new heart was working. Then he and Lower practised taking hearts out of dead bodies and putting them in again.

Using the techniques they had learned, Lower and Shumway made the first successful heart transplant, between two dogs. The only problem left, they felt, was **rejection** of the new heart by the body's **immune system**.

Surgeons carry out a heart transplant operation.

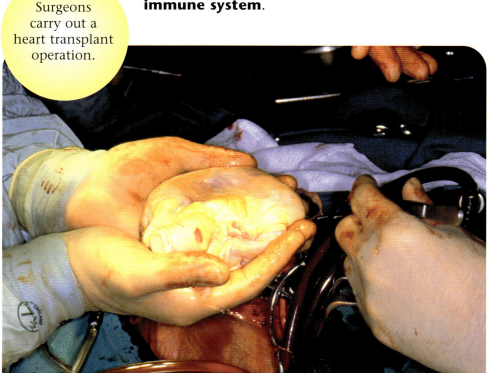

This diagram shows how a transplanted heart is usually attached. You can see the marks where it is stitched in.

superior vena cava

aorta

right atrium

The first heart transplant

In 1967, South African surgeon Christiaan Barnard decided to take a risk. He used Shumway and Lower's ideas to carry out the first human heart transplant. The patient was 55-year-old Louis Washansky. His new heart came from a young woman killed in a car crash. The operation took place in South Africa amid a blaze of publicity. The surgery went well. But Washansky's immune system was badly weakened by the drugs he was given to stop the new heart being rejected. He died 18 days later from pneumonia.

Nevertheless, the era of heart transplants had begun. The introduction of the drug **cyclosporine** 15 years later, in 1982, dramatically reduced the problem of rejection. Now thousands of hearts are transplanted successfully each year.

WHAT HAPPENS IN A HEART TRANSPLANT?

As soon as a **donor** dies, their heart is taken out. It is then kept cool in a special solution and taken to the patient. When it arrives, the patient is sent to sleep with **anaesthetic**. During the operation, the patient is kept alive on a heart machine that allows blood to bypass the patient's heart. Doctors cool the patient's heart and cut it out, except for the very back of the heart. They then sew in the new heart and connect up the blood vessels. As soon as the new heart warms up it should start beating, though it might need an electric shock to get the heart muscles pumping.

Electric hearts

Heart transplants now save a lot of people's lives, but there is a real shortage of donor hearts. In the late 1960s, medical scientists started trying to make a mechanical heart tiny enough to fit into the body. This would be very different from the giant machines they had used during operations.

THAT'S AMAZING!

Your heart is not much bigger than a fist. Yet it pumps over 9,000 litres (2,000 gallons) of blood a day. That is enough to fill 100 baths! And it goes on beating around once a second all your life. What is more, your heart's pumping rate varies all the time to suit the needs of your body. No wonder engineers have found it so hard to copy.

The Jarvik-7, an aluminium and plastic artificial heart, is powered by compressed air and electricity. It was named after its designer Robert Jarvik. It was first implanted in the United States, in 1982.

Your heart's main job is to pump blood. The idea was to swap it for a tiny pump made of metal and plastic. This would have flaps, moved by electric motors, to drive the blood through. But making an electric pump to replace the heart would need extraordinarily skilful engineering.

The first electric hearts were called "bridges". This was because they were only meant to keep the patient alive until a donor heart could be found. O.H. Frazier gave a patient this type of electric heart in Houston, in the United States, in 1969. Sadly, the patient did not live long enough for a donor to be found.

Electric heart for life

Meanwhile, many natural heart transplant patients were still dying because their new hearts were being rejected. Doctors wondered if electric hearts could be used permanently, not just as temporary bridges. An electric heart called the Jarvik-7 was developed. It was given to a number of dying patients in the early 1980s. One patient lived another two years.

The introduction of cyclosporine, in 1982, helped natural heart transplants avoid rejection. For a while, doctors lost interest in electric hearts, but the shortage of donors remained. Then, in 2001, a better and smaller electric heart, called the AbioCor, was given to a man called Robert Tools. Since then, a dozen more people have been given electric hearts. None of them have lived longer than a couple of months. But, without their electric hearts, they would have died in a few days. Each failure has also contributed to the gradual development of this technology.

? HOW LOUD IS AN ELECTRIC HEART?

Put your ear to someone's chest and you can hear their heart beating. You hear two sounds, "lub-DUB", as the heart valves open and close. You can feel the same beat running through your blood as a pulse by lightly touching your wrist. Most electric hearts pump the blood with a continuously whirring screw, so they have no beat or pulse. The first pumps clicked very noisily inside the patient's chest. Newer ones are almost silent.

Heart-lung transplants

Often, people who need heart transplants have damaged lungs as well. Because the lungs are wrapped around the heart in the chest, doctors wondered if they could transplant both at the same time.

Many heart-lung transplant candidates are born with the problem, so most of them are babies and young children. Without a transplant, all these children would die in less than a year or two. For this reason, doctors were determined to overcome the problems.

As long ago as the 1940s, Russian surgeon Vladimir Demikhov had performed heart-lung transplants on small animals such as puppies. However, he found that the donor lungs were quickly damaged if they were not given a blood supply within a few minutes.

Surgeons carry out Mary Gohlke's heart-lung transplant in 1981.

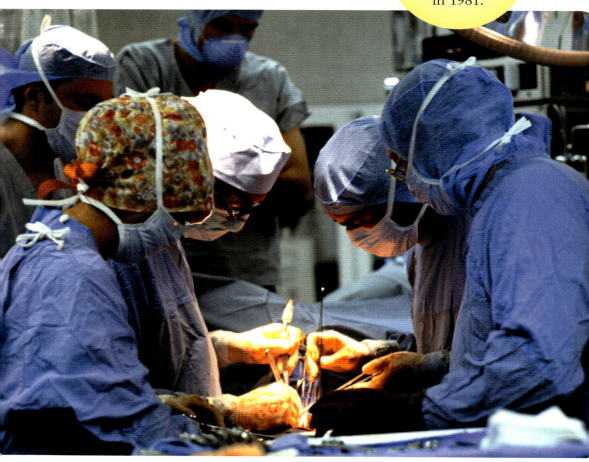

Moreover, with small animals, many of the **nerves** also needed to be transplanted, which made the task very difficult. As a result, the animals never survived long after the operation. In the 1970s, a surgeon called Aldo Castaneda was working in Minnesota, in the United States. His experiments showed that this was not such a problem with heart-lung transplants carried out on monkeys. Many of Castaneda's baboons survived for years after such a transplant. Doctors hoped that human heart-lung transplants might also be simpler than heart transplants. In 1968, just a year after the first heart transplant, American surgeon Denton Cooley performed the first heart-lung transplant, on a two-month-old baby. The baby survived just 14 hours after the operation.

The breakthrough

It was not until 1981 that doctors tried again. This time, the surgeons were Bruce Reitz and Norman Shumway of Stanford University, in the United States. Reitz thought the transplant was now worth trying because the discovery of cyclosporine (see page 29) made rejection less likely. The patient was 45-year-old advertising executive Mary Gohlke.

The operation was a success. Although the drugs used to combat rejection caused other problems, the transplant saved Mary and she is still alive today. Heart-lung transplants, often on tiny babies, are now fairly common. Between 800 and 1,000 are performed around the world each year. Nearly half the patients survive at least five years after their surgery.

TALKING SCIENCE

Major transplants are very traumatic for a patient, and there is no guarantee that the patient will live long after the operation. For these reasons, some people question whether they should be done. The first adult to receive a heart-lung transplant, Mary Gohlke, wrote a book afterwards called *I'll Take Tomorrow*. In it she writes, "*One thing is for certain; if Bruce Reitz came to me and said, 'Mary, something has gone wrong and we're going to have to do another double transplant,' I'd agree to it in a second.*"

Hands-on

With an **organ** transplant, there are only really **blood vessels** to reconnect. With a hand transplant, there are bones, tendons, and tiny **nerves** to join up too. By the late 1990s, transplanting organs of all kinds was becoming fairly common. But could surgeons ever succeed in transplanting hands?

Back in the 1920s, they had managed to reattach hands that had been accidentally cut off. Yet the hands were always left stiff and immovable. In the 1960s, Chinese surgeons showed how to reconnect nerves and tendons better. This meant that the patient often regained some movement in the hand.

Denis Chatelier, the world's first double hand and forearm transplant, holds a mobile telephone to demonstrate his progress a year after his operation.

? HOW IS A HAND TRANSPLANTED?

Hand transplant operations take 12 to 14 hours. First, the surgeons tie a band around the patient's arm to stop the blood flow. Then they cut back the skin to expose the parts they must connect. After that, they hold the transplant hand in place with a metal plate. Next, they stitch together first the tendons, then the nerves, and finally all the blood vessels, one by one. When all the connections are made, they take off the band around the arm. Blood starts to flow and the new hand changes from white to a pinkish colour. The surgeons finish the operation by folding back the skin to cover the join and sewing it in place.

Yet, so far, doctors had only reattached the patient's own hand. No one had yet tried attaching a **donor's** hand. For people who had lost a hand through disease, or whose severed hand was too damaged to reattach, transplanting a donor's hand was the only hope.

By the late 1990s, doctors had good drugs to stop transplants being **rejected**. In 1998, French surgeon Jean-Michel Dubernard tried a hand transplant on New Zealander Clint Hallam. Clint had lost his hand in a circular saw accident about 14 years earlier.

The operation went well, but there were problems (see "Clint Hallam's story" below). However, the following year, Matthew Scott in the United States was given a new hand. Then, in 2000, Dubernard transplanted both hands and forearms to Denis Chatelier, who had lost them in an explosion. Both men could soon move their new hands quite well.

CLINT HALLAM'S STORY

After 14 years without a hand, Clint Hallam felt uncomfortable with his new hand. It felt odd, and the anti-rejection drugs made him ill. Doctors say he stopped taking the drugs properly. Soon the hand began to be rejected by his body. Five months after the transplant, Hallam asked for it to be removed.

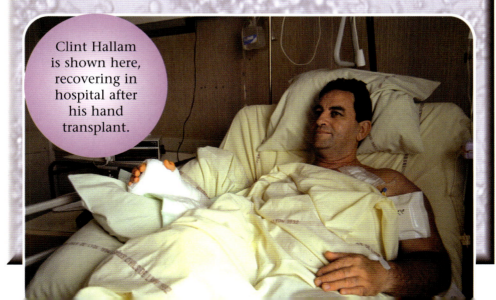

Clint Hallam is shown here, recovering in hospital after his hand transplant.

Face and head

We have seen some amazing breakthroughs in transplant surgery. Doctors can already transplant every **organ** as well as hands and limbs. Are there any limits to what they can swap in future? A partial face transplant has already been carried out, in France. One day it might even be possible to swap people's heads.

French surgeons hold a news conference in Lyon, France, in December 2005. Behind them, a computer-generated image shows details of the partial face transplant they performed on a French woman. Her nose, lips, and chin had been mauled by a dog.

Some people have terribly disfigured faces. Their faces may have been damaged by disease, or in an accident. For these people, having a damaged face is very distressing. Doctors already have the skills to give them a new, transplanted face.

Rebuilding faces

Over the last few decades, surgeons have gained great skill at moving skin and rebuilding parts of the body, especially the face. When this type of treatment involves rebuilding and remodelling body parts, it is called plastic surgery. Sometimes people have plastic surgery because of a very bad injury. Sometimes they have surgery because they want to look different in some way. For example, they may want to change the shape of their nose, or get rid of the bags under their eyes.

In 2003, there was a terrible accident in India. An 11-year-old girl's hair got caught in farm machinery, and her face was torn off. The surgeons were able to reattach it successfully.

Then, in 2004, doctors in Japan rebuilt the face of a man who had been badly burned. Six months before the operation, they started gradually inflating a balloon under the skin on his back. That way the skin became gradually separated, but was still alive. They were then able to take off a large piece to lay over his entire face, making holes for the eyes, nose, and mouth.

Transplanting faces

On 28 November 2005, a 38-year-old woman in France was given a partial face transplant. The patient's nose, lips, and chin had been badly damaged by a dog. The transplant was designed to replace part of her destroyed face with **tissue** from a **donor**. The donor was lying in a **coma** but was completely brain-dead.

Transplants such as these pose many problems. Firstly, there is the problem of **rejection**. Secondly, donors' families are worried about giving a loved one's face to another person. They are especially worried that the patient will end up looking like their loved one. Surgeons insist that the new face will have the patient's bone structure, so it will look like the patient rather than the donor. Nevertheless, surgeons are very wary of going ahead with this kind of operation.

JACQUELINE SABURIDO'S STORY

Early on the morning of 19 September 1999, 20-year-old Jacqueline Saburido was travelling home with friends from a birthday party near Austin, Texas, USA. Suddenly their car was hit head-on by another car, driven by a drunk driver, and burst into flames. Jacqui was burned over 60 per cent of her body. Even after 50 operations, her face is still very badly disfigured. She has shown tremendous courage and has become a major campaigner against drinking and driving. People like her hope that face transplants may soon be possible.

In 1818, Mary Shelley wrote *Frankenstein*, the most famous horror story of all time. She and her husband, Percy Shelley, were staying in Switzerland with the poet Lord Byron. One gloomy evening, Byron challenged his guests to come up with a scary story. Mary wrote about a brilliant young doctor called Victor Frankenstein, who made a creature from dead body parts, then brought it to life with electricity. Rejected by his creator, the creature turned to violence.

Head transplant?

There is no doubt that the most astonishing transplant would be an entire head, or an entire body, whichever way you look at it. Most doctors think it could never be done. Many people think it should never be done, even if it could be.

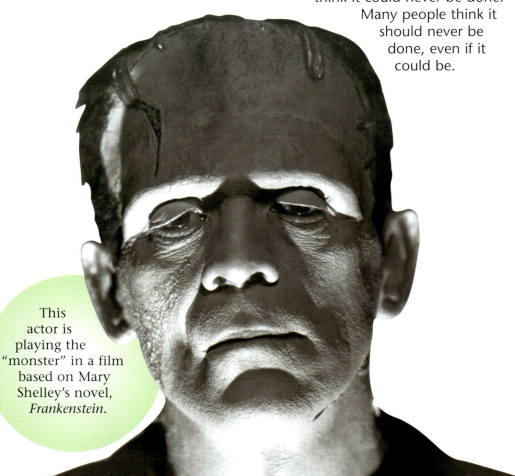

This actor is playing the "monster" in a film based on Mary Shelley's novel, *Frankenstein*.

All the same, one scientist, Professor Robert White, of Cleveland, Ohio, in the United States, has been carrying out head transplant experiments since the 1960s. In 1970, White cut off the head of a rhesus monkey and transplanted it to the body of another monkey. He connected up all the tissues and **blood vessels**, but not the **nerves**. Apparently, the monkey woke up, looked around, and even bit Professor White's finger. It died after eight days.

Since then, techniques have improved. In 1997, White conducted further experiments, and was able to keep monkeys with transplanted heads alive much longer. White insists that a human head transplant would be easier, because the blood vessels and tissues are much larger. Scientists already have the equipment needed to cool the head and stop the brain being damaged during the transplant. Crucially, though, a machine would need to keep blood flowing to the donor head.

The major obstacle, though, is that no one knows how to reattach nerves. Even if the surgeons were able to transplant the head, this means that its body would be completely paralysed.

Of course, the whole idea of a head transplant is very gruesome. Most doctors say it would be morally wrong. Others say it would raise a lot of legal and practical problems. It would be hard to say, for instance, who the person was, if they had one head and a different body. And who would be willing to give permission for their entire body to be used by someone else after they died?

WHAT IS QUADRIPLEGIA?

People might need a head transplant if they are paralysed from the neck down. Movement of the arms and legs depends on nerve signals being sent from the brain, through the spine. If the neck is injured, the spinal nerves may be damaged so badly that the signals cannot be sent. If this happens, the person can move neither their legs nor their arms. This is called quadriplegia.

Finding organs

The biggest problem facing transplant surgeons now is that there are just not enough **donor organs**. There are at least 180,000 people around the world who could be helped by a transplant. Yet there are only a few thousand suitable donor organs.

IS IT SAFE TO USE ANIMAL ORGANS?

A lot of people think it is simply wrong to use animals as a source of transplant organs. Also, many scientists are worried that pig organs might contain viruses that at present only infect pigs. If the organs are transplanted to humans they could infect humans, too. Because our bodies have never met these pig viruses before, our immune system might not recognize and fight them. These viruses could therefore prove deadly.

Some scientists think the answer may be to get donor organs from animals. But the problem is extreme **rejection**. Unless the **immune system** is suppressed with drugs, the body rejects organs from other humans. It rejects organs from animals very strongly indeed.

Now scientists think they might be able to beat this strong rejection. One idea is to use **genetic engineering** to disguise the **antigens** that mark the organ as non-human. For instance, scientists might put **genes** for human blood into pig embryos. Then, when the pigs grow up, their organs can be used for transplants. Because their blood has human antigens, scientists hope the pig's organs will not be rejected. Alternatively, they could remove the genes for alpha-gals. Alpha-gals are the antigens that identify a pig organ as non-human. In 2002, scientists **cloned** a pig called Goldie without alpha-gals.

These piglets were cloned by transplant researchers in Virginia, USA, in 2000.

Another way to beat strong rejection might be to use human stem cells. Human stem cells are the basic cells from which all our other cells develop. If these stem cells are introduced into a pig's organs, the organs may grow with human cells. Then it may seem so similar to a human organ that it might not be rejected by the human body. In 2003, scientists managed to get a kidney to grow in a mouse using human stem cells.

BABY FAE'S STORY

In 1984, Leonard Bailey transplanted a baboon heart into a baby known as Baby Fae. A baboon's heart is similar in size to a human baby's heart. Baby Fae was born with a poorly developed heart and was certain to die. Bailey gave her **cyclosporine** to try and prevent the heart being rejected. It did not work. Baby Fae died after 20 days, and doctors were put off using animal transplants for many years.

Man-made organs

Building mechanical organs is very difficult. It is hard enough to make a mechanical heart (see page 39). Yet the heart is really just a pump. Organs such as the kidneys and the liver have to carry out complex biochemical processes.

The best hope is **bioartificial organs**. These are plastic and metal machines that also include living cells. To create a bioartificial kidney, for instance, scientists take human kidney cells and give them nutrients. The cells are then put inside a **bioreactor**. A bioreactor is a container in which the cells are kept alive with oxygen and nutrients. It rotates in such a way that it fools the cells into thinking they are in a body. The bioreactor is then put inside a bigger plastic and metal machine. The machine works just like a **dialysis** machine (see page 25).

This is a bioartificial kidney unit working in a laboratory in Michigan, in the United States. Filtered blood flows along a tube into the canister, where kidney cells reabsorb essential blood elements.

? WHAT ARE STEM CELLS?

Stem cells are the basic cells from which all other cells in the body grow. They can grow into any kind of cell. The embryos from which babies develop are rich in stem cells. Adults have stem cells, too. They live quietly inside different tissues until they are needed, perhaps when the tissue is damaged and new cells are required to repair it. Scientists hope to use stem cells one day to help replace body parts that are damaged by disease or age.

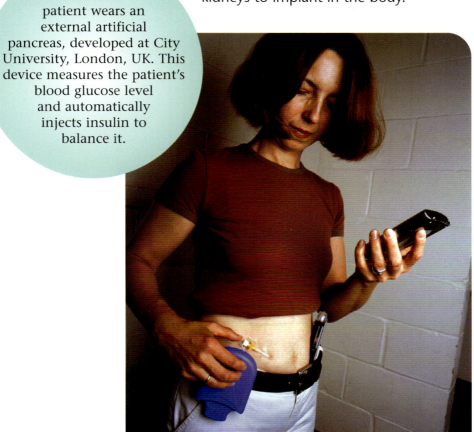

THAT'S AMAZING!

Instead of their regular injections and blood sugar checks, diabetics may one day have bioartificial **insulin** dispensers implanted into their bodies. The dispenser would automatically check their blood sugar levels and release exactly the right amount of insulin into their blood.

However, dialysis machines only do half the kidneys' work. They just filter out waste elements from the blood. They do not reclaim the essential elements and return them to the bloodstream the way real kidneys do. Scientists have been working on a better bioartificial kidney. They are taking stem cells from donor kidneys and using them to grow tube-shaped cells. These tubule cells do most of the kidneys' reclamation work. To grow them, hair-thin plastic fibres are coated with stem cells and put inside a small bioreactor. After about a week, the stem cells grow into tubule cells that can be used to make a bioartificial kidney.

Trials are under way to use bioartificial kidneys like these to replace normal dialysis machines. At present, they will only be used for short periods to help patients with kidney failure to survive until a transplant can be done. In the future, however, scientists hope to build tiny bioartificial kidneys to implant in the body.

A diabetic patient wears an external artificial pancreas, developed at City University, London, UK. This device measures the patient's blood glucose level and automatically injects insulin to balance it.

Growing new organs

At present, the only way to replace a failing organ is with a transplant from a donor, or with a specially constructed machine. But what if scientists could grow new organs? This process is called **tissue engineering**.

In one kind of tissue engineering, a damaged organ could actually repair itself. Using this technique, the tissue engineer injects a particular molecule, such as **human growth hormone**, into the damaged organ. The growth hormone then draws the patient's own body cells to the site and their own cells start to repair the damage.

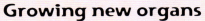

THAT'S AMAZING!

A couple in England are making themselves very unusual wedding rings. Tissue engineers are taking bone cell samples from their jawbones. The samples are then grown on a ring-shaped scaffold. These grow into a rough ring of bone, which is then sculpted to the couple's design.

Dr. David Mooney holds a tissue scaffold used to grow artificial human organs. The scaffold (in this case, a bandage) contains a network of special fibres. Cells from the patient's organ are placed on to the bandage, where they grow into the correct shape.

Another, more dramatic approach is to take stem cells from either the donor or the patient. These are then grown on a scaffold of plastic that will later dissolve inside the body. Similar materials are already used to make dissolvable stitches. The scaffold ensures that the cells grow in exactly the right shape.

When the cells are fully grown, the structure is transplanted into the damaged part of the body. Inside the body, the cells continue to grow, but they are helped by the body's own cells. In time, a brand new organ develops, called a neo-organ. The scaffold dissolves away, leaving the organ as good as new.

This artificial bone is made from a material that is very similar to natural bone. It allows stem cells, taken from the patient's bone marrow, to grow and develop into new bone tissue. The bioartificial bone can then be used in the patient's body to replace missing bone.

This technology might one day develop so far that no one ever needs a transplant. Whenever a body part fails or shows signs of damage, tissue engineers will step in and repair it. But this is a long way in the future.

WHAT'S HUMAN GROWTH HORMONE?

Human growth hormone (HGH) is a natural chemical made in your pituitary gland, deep inside your brain, behind your eyes. Your body produces HGH in short bursts, to trigger growth. It is made throughout your life, but especially when you are young and growing. Children who are not growing well may be given an HGH supplement, produced by **genetically engineered** bacteria.

Transplant surgery today and tomorrow

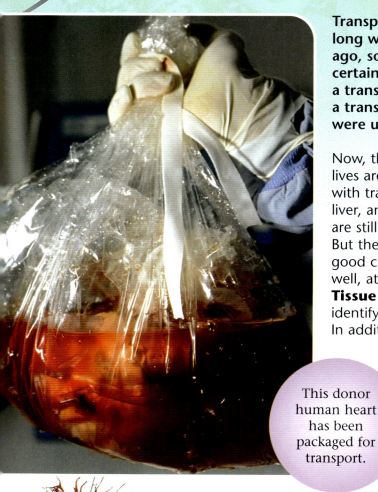

This donor human heart has been packaged for transport.

Transplants have come a long way. Just half a century ago, some patients would certainly have died without a transplant. Even with a transplant, many patients were unlikely to survive.

Now, thousands of people's lives are saved every year with transplants. Heart, lung, liver, and kidney transplants are still major operations. But the patient has a very good chance of getting well, at least for a few years. **Tissue typing** helps doctors identify suitable **organs**. In addition, drugs such as **cyclosporine** have reduced the chances of the transplanted organ being **rejected** by the patient.

? WHAT'S THE ORGAN TRADE?

The shortage of kidneys for transplant means that kidneys are worth a lot of money. Most people have two kidneys and can manage with just one. Many people in poor countries are desperate for cash. They can sell one of their own kidneys for US $5,000 or more. This means that people in poor countries sell a kidney, and are often made ill by it. Governments have done their best to stop the trade in organs. But people in rich countries are desperate to live, and people in poor countries are desperate for money, so it continues.

Sometimes organs are donated by close relatives, but many come from complete strangers. If the organ comes from someone who dies, it needs to be removed very soon after death. There is rarely time for doctors to contact the dead person's relatives to ask for permission to remove the organs. For this reason, health authorities urge people to carry a card with them at all times saying they are willing to donate their organs, if they should die.

The gift of life

The big problem remains the shortage of **donor** organs. Scientists are working on ways of overcoming this problem. New organs could be grown in animals, or in the laboratory by **tissue engineers**. Mechanical organs could be built from combinations of living cells and plastics. But all these developments are still some way off. In the meantime, people's lives depend on the generosity of those willing to donate their organs – after they die, or even while they are still alive.

A fairly common cause of death is road traffic accidents. If the victim is carrying an organ donor card, their organs can be used to save someone else's life.

Fifty years ago, surgeons watched helplessly as patients with failing organs died. Now remarkably, with a transplant, they can offer them hope.

Timeline

c.400 B.C. First skin graft performed in India by Susruta.

c.1580 First skin graft performed in Europe by Italian Gasparo Tagliacozzi.

1668 First successful bone graft by Dutchman Job van Meeneren.

1770s Laughing gas discovered by Joseph Priestley.

1819 First successful blood transfusion carried out by James Blundell.

1838 First transplant of the cornea of the eye performed on a gazelle by Richard Kissam.

1842 Crawford Long performs the first operation carried out under anaesthetic.

1846 First famous operation carried out under anaesthetic given by William Morton.

c.1875 First large skin graft carried out by Carl Thiersch.

1894 Alexis Carrel invents a way of stitching together blood vessels.

c.1900 First kidney transplants on dogs carried out by Emerich Ullmann and Alexis Carrel.

1901 Blood groups discovered by Karl Landsteiner.

1905 First successful human corneal transplant by Eduard Zirm.

1935 First mechanical heart built by Alexis Carrel and Charles Lindbergh.

1942 First use of curare as muscle relaxant for operations by Harold Griffiths.

1944 Peter Medawar discovers the idea of rejection of transplants.

1945 Willem Kolff builds the first kidney dialysis machine.

1948 Frank Macfarlane Burnet discovers that our bodies learn to recognize their own tissues.

1952 René Küss performs first human kidney transplant.

1954 Joseph Murray performs first successful human kidney transplant.

1950s Frank Macfarlane Burnet discovers how white blood cells and antibodies multiply to fight invaders.

1962 Roy Calne treats transplant patients with azathioprine to suppress rejection.

1963 Thomas Starzl combines azathioprine with steroids to suppress rejection in transplant patients.

1963 First liver transplants by Roy Calne and Thomas Starzl.

1963 First lung transplant by James Hardy.

1964 First transplant of animal heart to human by James Hardy.

1967 First kidney and pancreas transplant by Richard Lillehei.

1967 First human heart transplant by Christiaan Barnard.

1968 First heart and lung transplant by Denton Cooley.

1969 First implant of electric heart by O.H. Frazier.

1960s Tissue typing introduced to identify suitable donors.

1970 First animal head transplant by Robert White.

1981 First successful heart-lung transplant by Bruce Reitz.

1982 Cyclosporine introduced to suppress rejection.

1995 First transplantation of all internal organs except heart and lungs (i.e. kidney, pancreas, stomach, liver, intestine) by doctors in Miami, Florida, in the United States.

1998 First hand transplant carried out by Jean-Michel Dubernard.

2002 Goldie the pig is cloned to provide transplant organs.

2003 First tongue transplant performed in Vienna, in Austria.

2004 First ankle transplant by Sandro Giannini in Italy.

2005 First transplant of pancreas islet cells from living donor by surgeons in Kyoto, Japan.

2005 Partial face transplant carried out in France.

Biographies

These are some of the leading scientists in the story of transplant surgery.

Christiaan Barnard (1922–2001)

South African Christiaan Barnard became world-famous in 1967 when he performed the first human heart transplant in Cape Town, South Africa. He went on to perform double transplants, which meant placing a healthy heart alongside the patient's ill heart. He also pioneered the use of monkey hearts to keep patients alive while waiting for a suitable donor. Barnard was the son of a poor preacher. When one of his brothers died at the age of five from heart disease, Barnard decided to become a heart surgeon. His fame as a surgeon brought him celebrity and he was linked with some of the world's most beautiful women, including the Italian film actress Sophia Loren.

Roy Calne

Roy Calne was one of the pioneers of kidney transplants. Brought up in Surrey, in the United Kingdom, Calne was fascinated as a child with animals and engines. When he grew up he combined these two passions in his transplant work. In the 1950s, kidney transplants only worked between identical twins. In all other cases, the transplant was rejected. While working as a young surgeon in London, Calne had the idea of using the drug 6-mp to stop transplanted kidneys being rejected. In 1960, he went to the United States to work at the Peter Bent Brigham Hospital in Harvard. There he continued his transplant research work on dogs. Now, he used azathioprine. This drug is very similar to 6-mp but worked much better. Using azathioprine, Calne went on to perform some of the first successful kidney transplants on unrelated patients.

Alexis Carrel (1873–1944)

French-American Alexis Carrel was a great pioneer of transplants. He was born in Lyon, France. Here he did the first heart and kidney transplants on animals. He also developed a way of sewing blood vessels together, after seeing the French president Sadi-Carnot bleed to death from a stab wound. This technique, called the Carrel suture, is vital to transplant surgery today. In 1904, he moved to Canada, intending to become a cattle rancher. He later left Canada, and went to work at the Rockefeller Institute for Medical Research in New York. Here he did important work on organ transplants. In 1935, working with airman Charles Lindbergh, he constructed the first mechanical heart in order to keep patients alive while they underwent heart operations.

Karl Landsteiner (1868–1943)

Born in Vienna, Austria, Karl Landsteiner was a pioneer in the study of how our bodies combat disease. His greatest achievement was the discovery of blood groups. Until 1900, blood transfusions often failed. In 1901, Landsteiner showed that blood from one patient would often make the red blood cells of another patient clump together. He realized that this was because human blood is divided into different groups, and blood from different groups will not mix. Landsteiner originally thought there were just four blood groups (A, B, AB, and O). After he moved to New York in 1922, though, he discovered there were many more, including those with or without the Rhesus factor.

Peter Medawar (1915–1987)

Born in Brazil, Peter Medawar was the son of a Lebanese-British businessman. He became a zoologist in England. His greatest achievement, however, was discovering why transplants from another person usually failed. Horrified by the suffering of burns victims in the Second World War, he began experimenting with skin grafts on rabbits. He found that the body's immune system actually fights against the transplant. Medawar later found that in some cases foreign tissues may be tolerated. This is called immunological tolerance, and is crucial to transplants today.

William Morton (1819–1868)

William Morton is often called the "father of anaesthetics". He was brought up in Baltimore, in the United States, but went to work in Boston. There, in the Massachusetts General Hospital, Morton used fumes of ether to send patients to sleep during painful operations. Ether fumes are made by mixing acid and alcohol. Morton placed a sponge soaked with alcohol into a bottle with two necks, and put drops of acid in through one neck. The patient breathed in the fumes through the other. It worked so well that, in 1846, Morton sent a patient to sleep with ether while a tumour was cut out of his neck. Three weeks later, Morton used ether to send a patient to sleep while her leg was amputated. From then on, even the most severe operations could be carried out without the patient feeling anything.

Thomas Starzl

Thomas Starzl was born in Iowa, in the United States, in 1926, and trained as a doctor in Chicago. He is one of the world's great transplant surgeons. He performed some of the most successful early kidney transplants. The key to his success was his idea of using steroid drugs whenever a patient showed signs of rejecting a transplant. Starzl then went on to lead the way in introducing the important drug cyclosporine for transplant patients. He also pioneered liver transplants.

59

Glossary

amputation operation to remove a diseased body part, usually a limb

anaesthetic drug used to numb pain or to make the patient unconscious during an operation

antibiotic medicine that can kill bacteria but not viruses

antibody protein particle in the body that identifies and attacks germs

antigen protein marker that makes the body's defences recognize a cell as foreign

artery large blood vessel that carries blood from the heart to the rest of the body

azathioprine drug that stops cells multiplying. First used against childhood cancer and later to fight transplant rejection by stopping white blood cells multiplying.

bioartificial organ organ transplanted into a patient that combines living cells with plastic and metal parts

bioreactor special container in which living cells are grown

blood group one of the different types into which human blood is divided

blood vessel tiny small tube that carries blood around the body

clone produce an identical copy of a living thing

coma state of deep unconsciousness that can sometimes continue indefinitely

cornea clear layer that covers the surface of the eye

cyclosporine drug used to suppress the body's defences and reduce the chances of a transplant being rejected

dialysis process in which waste is filtered from the blood. This process is usually performed by the kidney, but may be performed by a machine outside the body.

donor person or animal that provides an organ or tissue for transplant

gene part of the material inside every cell that gives a particular characteristic to a living thing. A gene is passed on from parent to offspring.

genetically engineered when a living thing has its genetic material artificially altered

graft piece of skin or other tissue taken from one part of the body and placed elsewhere in the body to replace a damaged piece of skin or tissue

hormone substance that triggers certain processes in the body

human growth hormone natural body chemical that triggers growth

human leukocyte antigen (HLA) special marker protein on the coating of most cells in the body

immune system all the body's defences against disease and infection

immunological tolerance when the body accepts foreign tissue

immunosuppressant drug drug used to reduce the power of the body's defences

inflammation swelling and redness caused by an infection

insulin hormone produced by the body that controls the amount of sugar in the blood. It does this by allowing cells to take in the sugar they need for energy.

lymphocyte type of white blood cell that helps identify and destroy particular germs in the body

macrophage type of white blood cell that swallows up invading cells

nerve fibre that sends information around the body, such as pain, or other signals from the senses

organ soft, complex body part, such as the heart or liver, which has a particular task in the body

plasma liquid part of the blood

polio disease, caused by a virus, that can result in paralysis

rejection way in which the body's defence system attacks transplants

retina area at the back of the eye that receives light and sends nerve signals to the brain

Rhesus factor protein marker that some people have on their red blood cells. Those that have this marker are Rhesus positive.

steroid drug that suppresses the body's defences and reduces redness and swelling

sutures stitches that surgeons use to hold body parts together while they heal naturally

tissue natural materials in the body, such as bone, blood, and muscle

tissue engineering growing new tissues and organs from living cells on a plastic framework that eventually dissolves

tissue typing testing cells in the blood of transplant donors to see how closely their blood matches the patient's blood

tumour cancerous growth

transfusion process carried out when a patient is given some of someone else's blood

vein blood vessel that carries blood back to the heart

white blood cell large, pale-coloured, blood cell that plays an important role in the body's defence system

Further resources

If you have enjoyed this book and want to find out more, you can look at the following books and websites.

Books

Body: An Amazing Tour of Human Anatomy
Robert Winston
(Dorling Kindersley, 2005)

The Immune System: Injury, Illness and Death (Body Focus)
Carol Ballard
(Heinemann Library, 2004)

Incredible Body
illlustrated by Stephen Biesty
(Dorling Kindersley, 1997)

Pig-heart Boy
Malorie Blackman
(Corgi, 1999)

A Painful History of Medicine: Scalpels, Stitches and Scars – A History of Surgery
John Townsend
(Raintree, 2005)

Websites

Transplant kids
www.transplantkids.co.uk
A fun and informative website set up and run by a family with a transplant child. Full of information about transplants, personal stories of transplant patients, a chat room to air your views on transplants, and links to other useful sites.

Transplants in mind
www.timeinmind.co.uk
Transplants in mind is a charity that tries to encourage people to become donors.

Transplant adventure camps for kids
www.tackers.org
TACKERS are adventure camps that bring together children from around the world who have had transplants.

TalkTransplant
www.talktransplant.com/ Home.aspx
This site provides information about organ transplant for patients, their families, and their carers. The site contains in-depth information on heart transplant, liver transplant, lung transplant, and kidney transplant operations.

Transplant friends
www.pazl.com/transplant
A website linking people who have been through transplants.

British Heart Foundation
www.bhf.org.uk/yheart
The British Heart Foundation's site for teenagers.

Index

Index